coffee

/ˈkɒfi/

noun

1. 1.

a hot drink made from the roasted and ground seeds (coffee beans) of a tropical shrub.

"a cup of coffee"

synonyms:

joe, java

the shrub which yields coffee seeds, native to the Old World tropics.

CPSIA information can be obtained
at www.ICGtesting.com
Printed in the USA
BVHW020758190419
545902BV00023B/115/P